Intimate Times

of

Revelations

Intimate Times of Revelations

Donell Givens

All primary Scripture were taken from the New King James Version of the Holy Bible. Secondary Scripture (in italics) were taken from the Amplified Version of the Holy Bible.

Published by CLF PUBLISHING, LLC. 3281 Guasti Road, Seventh Floor, Ontario, CA 91761.
(760) 669-8149.

Copyright © 2011 by Donell Givens. All rights reserved. No portion of this book may be reproduced, stored in a retrieval system, or transmitted by any form or any means electronically, photocopied, recorded, or any other except for brief quotations in printed reviews, without the prior permission of the publisher.

Cover Design by Senir Design. Contact information-
info@senirdesign.com.

ISBN # 978-0-9899408-5-6

Printed in the United States of America.

Dedication

I dedicate this book to my wife who lovingly encouraged me to keep going.

Additionally, I dedicate this book to Bishop Leon Martin, his lovely wife, Dr. Jacqueline Martin and to all the members of Love, Peace, and Happiness Family Christian Fellowship Church. You guys have been so kind and encouraging to me. Through your ministry, I have been able to preach the gospel, teach Bible College, co-write a play, and then act in the same play. I was also used as an orator. With a heart that is filled with gratitude and love, I dedicate this book to all of you. May God richly bless you for all your kindness that you have shown to my wife and me.

Acknowledgements

The first person I would like to acknowledge is Sister Geraldine Kyles. It was her persistence that got the ball rolling on writing a book in the first place. Every time I would share different things that the Lord would reveal to me, her response was always the same, "Brother, you need to write a book." Her encouragement would always ring in my heart. Yet, I would continually not get started over and over again. One day in between church services, Sister Kyles called a dear friend, Dr. Cassundra White-Elliott, over to the place that we were standing. She said, "Our brother needs to write a book. Can you help him?"

This brings me to the next person I would like to acknowledge, Dr. Cassundra White-Elliott, my publisher. Dr. Cassundra is the person you need on your side if you want to keep moving toward the thing you say you want to do. I don't really think there would have been a book without her help. She simply willed this book into existence. I really appreciate her help.

I acknowledge Dr. Jacqueline Martin for her encouraging words.

Finally, I acknowledge my younger sister Carletha Montgomery who has been a great encourager.

Donell Givens

Introduction

Sometimes it is good to allow God to speak to us in the early morning when everyone has not yet awakened to see the dawning of the new day that is ahead of them, or in the evening at the end of a busy day when everyone has gone to sleep.

There have even been times while at work on a break when God has shared something with me that could benefit me or someone else.

In the early days when I had these encounters, I wouldn't pay much attention to them, or I would try to remember them later, but they would have faded away never to be recaptured.

Now, I find it beneficial to write down some of the things God speaks into my spirit to capture those moments or seconds on paper.

After sharing some of the things God had given me, I found that they were not only a blessing to me, but also to those who took the time to listen to the insights that God had given me. After the urgings of several people and the prompting in my spirit, I thought it would be a good idea to broaden those moments to a larger audience. As a result, this book *Intimate Times of Revelations* was born.

After each passage of God's revelation, I have included space for you to write the things that God places on your heart as the still small voice of the Holy Spirit speaks to you.

Sometime in the future, I am going to write a book filled with intuitive revelations from God, but for now, I want you to experience the joy of just capturing revelations from God yourself. I have been told that when you want to draw water from a well that has not been in use for a while, you simply must prime or wet the pump before you start the process of pumping up the underground water.

This book is designed to get you in a place where you to will begin to write down the things that you hear, so they will not simply fade away over time. My prayer for you is that after you have taken this thirty-day journey, your ability to hear and write down those insightful nuggets you receive from time to time will begin or be increased. I am sure that once you learn this discipline, you as well as others will be blessed with the things that God will show you on your journey.

Well, without any further ado, I will simply say, "May God bless you on your journey, and enjoy your trip."

REVELATIONS FROM THE LORD

DAY ONE

Matt 7:14

Because narrow *is* the gate and difficult *is* the way which leads to life, and there are few who find it.

But the gate is narrow (contracted by pressure) and the way is straitened and compressed that leads away to life, and few are those who find it.

Time is a road we travel on in life. The word of God is our map that will lead us to the place of God. The Holy Spirit keeps us on course and makes sure we read our maps correctly, so we don't get the directions confused. The Father speaks into our hearts to make sure we don't forget why we got on the road in the first place.

Your thoughts for today:

DAY TWO

Hebrews 11:1-3

Now faith is the substance of things hoped for, the evidence of things not seen. For by it the elders obtained a *good* testimony. By faith we understand that the worlds were framed by the word of God, so that the things which are seen were not made of things which are visible.

NOW FAITH is the assurance (the confirmation, the title deed) of the things [we] hope for, being the proof of things [we] do not see and the conviction of their reality [faith perceiving as real fact what is not revealed to the senses]. For by [faith-trust and holy fervor born of faith] the men of old had divine testimony borne to them and obtained a good report. By faith we understand that the worlds [during the successive ages] were framed (fashioned, put in order, and equipped for their intended purpose) by the word of God, so that what we see was not made out of things which are visible.

Faith is the antidote to any challenge the enemy could ever bring your way. Faith, which is merely trusting God's word, operates like shocks on a car. The better the shocks, the less you feel the bumps in life.

Your thoughts for today:

DAY THREE

Proverbs 3:5-6

Trust in the LORD with all your heart, And lean not on your own understanding; In all your ways acknowledge Him, And He shall direct your paths.

Lean on, trust in, and be confident in the Lord with all your heart and mind and do not rely on your own insight or understanding. In all your ways know, recognize, and acknowledge Him, and He will direct and make straight and plain your paths.

Thinking positively has some benefits and even brings some long term advantages. However, to have a positive disposition apart from God and to merely have the encouragement of a motivational concept in the arena of the mind alone is totally incomplete for a Christian. A child of God is not limited to the mind alone for he/she operates in the realm of the spirit, which is superior to the mind and is unlimited in its operation.

Your thoughts for today:

_____
_____
_____
_____
_____
_____
_____
_____
_____
_____
_____
_____

DAY FOUR

John 6:63

It is the Spirit who gives life; the flesh profits nothing. The words that I speak to you are spirit, and *they* are life.

It is the Spirit Who gives life [He is the Life-giver]; the flesh conveys no benefit whatever [there is no profit in it]. The words (truths) that I have been speaking to you are spirit and life.

The person or persons who speak into your life determine the structure, if you will, of your spiritual DNA. Those that you allow into your ear gates have been given access into your heart. Your heart is the place where genuine change or reshaping will occur. When that voice speaks the truth of God, illumination will give birth to revelation. As revelation expands and increases, darkness and fear will decrease, and true deliverance will embrace your life.

Your thoughts for today:

_____
_____
_____
_____
_____
_____
_____
_____
_____
_____

DAY FIVE

Psalms 88:1-2

O LORD, God of my salvation, I have cried out day and night before You. Let my prayer come before You; Incline Your ear to my cry.

O LORD, the God of my salvation, I have cried to You for help by day; at night I am in Your presence. Let my prayer come before You and really enter into Your presence; incline Your ear to my cry!

Many people stand back and admire people that seem to have an awesome relationship with God. Those are the people they look for when they have something going on in their lives and they need to get a prayer through. That in itself is not a bad thing, yet God would really like for you to be that person.

Your thoughts for today:

DAY SIX

Proverbs 13:20

He who walks with wise *men* will be wise,
But the companion of fools will be destroyed.

He who walks [as a companion] with wise men is wise, but he who associates with [self-confident] fools is [a fool himself and] shall smart for it.

One of the best ways to avoid backsliding is to walk with people that have a passion for the Lord. If you walk with people on fire for God, the sparks of their lives will keep you ignited as well. What you are around is what you will become. Success in God can be assured by the company one keeps.

Your thoughts for today:

DAY SEVEN

1 Peter 2:9-10

But you *are* a chosen generation, a royal priesthood, a holy nation, His own special people, that you may proclaim the praises of Him who called you out of darkness into His marvelous light; who once *were* not a people but *are* now the people of God, who had not obtained mercy but now have obtained mercy.

But you are a chosen race, a royal priesthood, a dedicated nation, [God's] own purchased, special people, that you may set forth the wonderful deeds and display the virtues and perfections of Him Who called you out of darkness into His marvelous light. Once you were not a people [at all], but now you are God's people; once you were unpitied, but now you are pitied and have received mercy.

It is our understanding about who we are in God that will free us from the misconception of the box that others may try to place us in. It is that same understanding that will cause us to mount up with wings of eagles. When we see ourselves seated in heavenly places in Christ Jesus, we will begin to look at our circumstances from an elevated position. Then the size of our problems will seem smaller and defeatable. We will have the ability in God to crush what is trying to crush us.

Your thoughts for today:

DAY EIGHT

2 Cor. 4:17-18
For our light affliction, which is but for a moment, is working for us a far more exceeding *and* eternal weight of glory, while we do not look at the things which are seen, but at the things which are not seen. For the things which are seen *are* temporary, but the things which are not seen *are* eternal.

For our light, momentary affliction (this slight distress of the passing hour) is ever more and more abundantly preparing and producing and achieving for us an everlasting weight of glory [beyond all measure, excessively surpassing all comparisons and all calculations, a vast and transcendent glory and blessedness never to cease!], Since we consider and look not to the things that are seen but to the things that are unseen; for the things that are visible are temporal (brief and fleeting), but the things that are invisible are deathless and everlasting.

2 Cor. 5:7
For we walk by faith, not by sight.

For we walk by faith [we regulate our lives and conduct ourselves by our conviction or belief respecting man's relationship to God and divine things, with trust and holy fervor; thus we walk] not by sight or appearance.

Never let what you see naturally out weigh what you hear supernaturally. The limitation of natural sight, when allowed to, can dismantle the purpose of God in your life because it breeds doubt and unbelief.

Your thoughts for today:

DAY NINE

James 1:6-7

But let him ask in faith, with no doubting, for he who doubts is like a wave of the sea driven and tossed by the wind. For let not that man suppose that he will receive anything from the Lord.

Only it must be in faith that he asks with no wavering (no hesitating, no doubting). For the one who wavers (hesitates, doubts) is like the billowing surge out at sea that is blown hither and thither and tossed by the wind. For truly, let not such a person imagine that he will receive anything [he asks for] from the Lord.

Doubt and unbelief are enemies of your faith in God. Without faith, you only have your own natural abilities. As good as they may be, they cannot produce the miraculous power of the living God. The limitations of natural ability cannot reach the limitless boundaries of the impossible.

Your thoughts for today:

_____
_____
_____
_____
_____
_____
_____
_____
_____
_____
_____
_____
_____
_____

DAY TEN

James 2:8-9

If you really fulfill *the* royal law according to the Scripture, *"You shall love your neighbor as yourself,"* you do well; but if you show partiality, you commit sin, and are convicted by the law as transgressors.

If indeed you [really] fulfill the royal Law in accordance with the Scripture, You shall love your neighbor as [you love] yourself, you do well. But if you show servile regard (prejudice, favoritism) for people, you commit sin and are rebuked and convicted by the Law as violators and offenders.

We can have a loving hug for those that smell like us. We are kind to those that have been privileged in society with wealth or position, but we look over those who may not have a home or nice clothes. We turn our noses up at those that don't fit our standards in life, yet we stick our chests out and call ourselves Christians. Saints of the Most High God, this should not be.

Your thoughts for today:

_____
_____
_____
_____
_____
_____
_____
_____
_____
_____
_____
_____
_____

DAY ELEVEN

Hebrews 12:1-2

Therefore we also, since we are surrounded by so great a cloud of witnesses, let us lay aside every weight, and the sin which so easily ensnares *us,* and let us run with endurance the race that is set before us, looking unto Jesus, the author and finisher of *our* faith, who for the joy that was set before Him endured the cross, despising the shame, and has sat down at the right hand of the throne of God.

THEREFORE THEN, since we are surrounded by so great a cloud of witnesses [who have borne testimony to the Truth], let us strip off and throw aside every encumbrance (unnecessary weight) and that sin which so readily (deftly and cleverly) clings to and entangles us, and let us run with patient endurance and steady and active persistence the appointed course of the race that is set before us, Looking away [from all that will distract] to Jesus, Who is the Leader and the Source of our faith [giving the first incentive for our belief] and is also its Finisher [bringing it to maturity and perfection]. He, for the joy [of obtaining the prize] that was set before Him, endured the cross, despising and ignoring the shame, and is now seated at the right hand of the throne of God.

Sometimes like a fishing line caught on the rocks that doesn't allow the fisherman to fish or to bring in what was caught, our thoughts, past hurts, and unforgiveness do not allow us to receive answers, solutions and directional insight from God.

Your thoughts for today:

_____
_____
_____
_____
_____
_____
_____
_____
_____
_____
_____
_____
_____
_____
_____
_____

DAY TWELVE

Isaiah 1:19

If you are willing and obedient, You shall eat the good of the land.

If you are willing and obedient, you shall eat the good of the land.

It is obedience that is the key to the door of the promises of God. The willing obedience of the Children of God will assure and secure the blessings of God into their lives. Many have a feign love toward God that is predicated upon His answer to their prayers, but when the answer to the prayer is "No, not yet," their hearts wax cold toward Him. Conditional love is not love at all, but an attempt to manipulate.

Your thoughts for today:

_____
_____
_____
_____
_____
_____
_____
_____
_____
_____
_____
_____

DAY THIRTEEN

Matthew 5:16

Let your light so shine before men, that they may see your good works and glorify your Father in heaven.

Let your light so shine before men that they may see your moral excellence and your praiseworthy, noble, and good deeds and recognize and honor and praise and glorify your Father Who is in heaven.

The level of light we reflect is predicated on the amount of light to which we are exposed. Our exposure of light is determined by our decision to walk in the light. Light has to do with revealed understanding of God and His Word, which is another word for revelation. The more revelation we receive, the greater our ability to walk with God who is the source of all light and life.

Your thoughts for today:

_____
_____
_____
_____
_____
_____
_____
_____
_____
_____
_____
_____
_____

DAY FOURTEEN

John 8:31-32

Then Jesus said to those Jews who believed Him, "If you abide in My word, you are My disciples indeed. And you shall know the truth, and the truth shall make you free."

So Jesus said to those Jews who had believed in Him, If you abide in My word [hold fast to My teachings and live in accordance with them], you are truly My disciples. And you will know the Truth, and the Truth will set you free.

Truth is like a wall that can stand alone without the support of any other wall, so to walk in truth is to bring balance into your life, but to live on a foundation of lies is like being a drunk man getting off a roller coaster and not expecting to fall. Jesus says, "I am the way, the truth and the life."

Your thoughts for today:

DAY FIFTEEN

Romans 8:28

And we know that all things work together for good to those who love God, to those who are the called according to *His* purpose.

We are assured and know that [God being a partner in their labor] all things work together and are [fitting into a plan] for good to and for those who love God and are called according to [His] design and purpose.

Many times we don't understand the things God has allowed or orchestrated in our lives. Sometimes, they seem beyond our ability to understand or to endure, yet God like a master chef knows all the ingredients, temperature and time needed to bring us into our prescribed destiny. Our responsibility is just to trust the process.

Your thoughts for today:

DAY SIXTEEN

1 John 4:20

If someone says, "I love God," and hates his brother, he is a liar; for he who does not love his brother whom he has seen, how can he love God whom he has not seen?

If anyone says, I love God, and hates (detests, abominates) his brother [in Christ], he is a liar; for he who does not love his brother, whom he has seen, cannot love God, Whom he has not seen.

Genuinely authentic love for God is weighed on the balance scales of how much you love people. The greater your love for people, the greater the weight or the more valid your saying or voicing your love for God will become.

Your thoughts for today:

DAY SEVENTEEN

Isaiah 61:3b

That they may be called trees of righteousness, The planting of the LORD, that He may be glorified."

That they may be called oaks of righteousness [lofty, strong, and magnificent, distinguished for uprightness, justice, and right standing with God], the planting of the Lord, that He may be glorified.

The best way to sooth a heavy heart is to give God praise. God inhabits the praises of His people. When we lift up the name of the Lord, He will lift the burden we carry in our hearts. The enemy will always attempt to keep our minds stuck in a negative rut, but praise will take us from the valley to the mountain top.

Your thoughts for today:

DAY EIGHTEEN

1 Peter 5:6

Therefore humble yourselves under the mighty hand of God, that He may exalt you in due time.

Therefore humble yourselves [demote, lower yourselves in your own estimation] under the mighty hand of God, that in due time He may exalt you.

Each man must go through the seasons God has ordained for him. God sets the temperature and the time. God ordains the process. Go along for the ride, and you will end up at the right place at the right time. Surrender is the best pathway for success in God. Seasons in life act like gear shifters that bring you to people, places and circumstances designed by God to bring you into your destiny.

Your thoughts for today:

_____
_____
_____
_____
_____
_____
_____
_____
_____
_____
_____
_____

DAY NINETEEN

John 14:6

Jesus said to him, "I am the way, the truth, and the life. No one comes to the Father except through Me.

Jesus said to him, I am the Way and the Truth and the Life; no one comes to the Father except by (through) Me.

People have been searching for truth for generations. Many have embraced what appeared to be truth only to find that the closer they got to that truth or the deeper they dug into the root of it, the more they were unsure of its authenticity. It is hard to find genuine truth without God because God is the embodiment of all truth.

Your thoughts for today:

_____
_____
_____
_____
_____
_____
_____
_____
_____
_____
_____
_____
_____

DAY TWENTY

Daniel 11:32b

But the people who know their God shall be strong, and carry out *great exploits*.

But the people who know their God shall prove themselves strong and shall stand firm and do exploits [for God].

Many want the benefit of knowing God without the experience of knowing Him. They want to declare His name and cause mountains to move, but they don't know Him by name. Some people are looking for physical manifestations without supernatural revelation. This can never be. People must come to God if they want the benefit of knowing Him.

Your thoughts for today:

_____
_____
_____
_____
_____
_____
_____
_____
_____
_____
_____
_____

DAY TWENTY-ONE

I Cor. 2:9-11

But as it is written: *"Eye has not seen, nor ear heard, Nor have entered into the heart of man The things which God has prepared for those who love Him."* But God has revealed *them* to us through His Spirit. For the Spirit searches all things, yes, the deep things of God. For what man knows the things of a man except the spirit of the man which is in him? Even so no one knows the things of God except the Spirit of God.

But, on the contrary, as the Scripture says, What eye has not seen and ear has not heard and has not entered into the heart of man, [all that] God has prepared (made and keeps ready) for those who love Him [who hold Him in affectionate reverence, promptly obeying Him and gratefully recognizing the benefits He has bestowed]. Yet to us God has unveiled and revealed them by and through His Spirit, for the [Holy] Spirit searches diligently, exploring and examining everything, even sounding the profound and bottomless things of God [the divine counsels and things hidden and beyond man's scrutiny].

For what person perceives (knows and understands) what passes through a man's thoughts except the man's own spirit within him? Just so no one discerns (comes to know and comprehend) the thoughts of God except the Spirit of God.

Don't expect for people to understand what God is doing in your life. The further you travel in the Spirit, the less people will understand the things that you do in God. Sometimes God is just calling you into a deeper walk into His will and purpose for your life.

Your thoughts for today:

DAY TWENTY-TWO

Romans 8:14-16

For as many as are led by the Spirit of God, these are sons of God. For you did not receive the spirit of bondage again to fear, but you received the Spirit of adoption by whom we cry out, "Abba, Father." The Spirit Himself bears witness with our spirit that we are children of God.

For all who are led by the Spirit of God are sons of God. For [the Spirit which] you have now received [is] not a spirit of slavery to put you once more in bondage to fear, but you have received the Spirit of adoption [the Spirit producing sonship] in [the bliss of] which we cry, Abba (Father)! Father! The Spirit Himself [thus] testifies together with our own spirit, [assuring us] that we are children of God.

When we consider the faithfulness of God, it should cause our fears to subside and drift into a place of obscurity. After all, most of the things we fear most never even happen. We should always remember that God, the sustainer of all life, will never leave or forsake us. He will keep us in the hollow of His hand. His love for us is our greatest weapon in times of adversity.

Your thoughts for today:

DAY TWENTY-THREE

Jeremiah 33:3

'Call to Me, and I will answer you, and show you great and mighty things, which you do not know.'

Call to Me and I will answer you and show you great and mighty things, fenced in and hidden, which you do not know (do not distinguish and recognize, have knowledge of and understand).

God is enough. Have you ever heard people tell you that all they have is God, as if having Him was somehow inferior to the many other things someone else had minus Him? What about the believer that says he/she had to give up so much in order to have a relationship with God. Sometimes, we don't really understand just how awesome it is to have a relationship with the true and the living God. "Lord, open our eyes to see and understand the wonder of just how great you are."

Your thoughts for today:

_____
_____
_____
_____
_____
_____
_____
_____
_____

DAY TWENTY-FOUR

Psalms 22:3

But You *are* holy, Enthroned in the praises of Israel.

But You are holy, O You Who dwell in [the holy place where] the praises of Israel [are offered].

The best place to hear the voice of God is in the midst of praise and worship. That is the place where the sounds of the enemy and the world system are silenced. When you really want a word from God, release praise and worship especially when you don't feel like it because that is when you offer up the sacrifice of praise.

Your thoughts for today:
___
___
___
___
___
___
___
___
___
___
___
___
___
___

DAY TWENTY-FIVE

John 3:16

For God so loved the world that He gave His only begotten Son, that whoever believes in Him should not perish but have everlasting life.

For God so greatly loved and dearly prized the world that He [even] gave up His only begotten (unique) Son, so that whoever believes in (trusts in, clings to, relies on) Him shall not perish (come to destruction, be lost) but have eternal (everlasting) life.

The key to your success in God is love for others. Humility is the birthing place of love. This is the place where you place someone else's concerns above your own. Yes, this is the place of giving. When we give love, we act like God and both parties are blessed: the giver and the receiver.

Your thoughts for today:
_____
_____
_____
_____
_____
_____
_____
_____
_____
_____
_____
_____
_____
_____
_____

DAY TWENTY-SIX

Galatians 5:6

For in Christ Jesus neither circumcision nor uncircumcision avails anything, but faith working through love.

For [if we are] in Christ Jesus, neither circumcision nor uncircumcision counts for anything, but only faith activated and energized and expressed and working through love.

True love is a matter of faith because real love is not a condition of the soul but of the spirit. True love dwells in the spirit but is expressed through the vessel of the soul and then released through the expression of the body. True love operates by faith, but is greater than the faith that is needed to produce it. True love is the expression of God.

Your thoughts for today:

_____
_____
_____
_____
_____
_____
_____
_____
_____
_____
_____
_____
_____

DAY TWENTY-SEVEN

Isaiah 43:1-3

But now, thus says the LORD, who created you, O Jacob, And He who formed you, O Israel: "Fear not, for I have redeemed you; I have called *you* by your name; You *are* Mine. When you pass through the waters, I *will be* with you; And through the rivers, they shall not overflow you. When you walk through the fire, you shall not be burned, Nor shall the flame scorch you. For I *am* the LORD your God, The Holy One of Israel, your Savior; I gave Egypt for your ransom, Ethiopia and Seba in your place."

BUT NOW [in spite of past judgments for Israel's sins], thus says the Lord, He Who created you, O Jacob, and He Who formed you, O Israel: Fear not, for I have redeemed you [ransomed you by paying a price instead of leaving you captives]; I have called you by your name; you are Mine. When you pass through the waters, I will be with you, and through the rivers, they will not overwhelm you. When you walk through the fire, you will not be burned or scorched, nor will the flame kindle upon you. For I am the Lord your God, the Holy One of Israel, your Savior; I give Egypt [to the Babylonians] for your ransom, Ethiopia and Seba [a province of Ethiopia] in exchange [for your release].

Life will many times have turns and valleys, pits and mountains, yet each place that we find ourselves in is just a part of the obstacle course for victory.

Your thoughts for today:

DAY TWENTY-EIGHT

Genesis 2:7

And the LORD God formed man *of* the dust of the ground, and breathed into his nostrils the breath of life; and man became a living being.

Then the Lord God formed man from the dust of the ground and breathed into his nostrils the breath or spirit of life, and man became a living being.

Oh the wonder of God, so kind, so loving, mercifully forgiving and patient. Who wouldn't take some time and bless the One that spoke and created all we see or will ever see? Who wouldn't blow kisses at the One that blew into us and caused what was lifeless to move and have its being?

Your thoughts for today:

DAY TWENTY-NINE

Ecclesiastes 3:1

To everything *there is* a season,
A time for every purpose under heaven.

TO EVERYTHING there is a season, and a time for every matter or purpose under heaven.

To truly know God can only happen for those who would dare to spend enough time with Him. Isn't it interesting to note that most of us have no problem with giving our attention or time to almost any venture except God? How much time do we give to work or friends and family? How much time do we give to television or games or so many other nearly meaningless things that really add little or nothing valuable to our lives? Why are we standing God up and placing Him on the shelf of our lives until we need Him again? What would happen if He were to simply ignore us just for a day? I wonder if we could even survive.

Your thoughts for today:

_____
_____
_____
_____
_____
_____
_____
_____

DAY THIRTY

1 John 5:14-15

Now this is the confidence that we have in Him, that if we ask anything according to His will, He hears us. And if we know that He hears us, whatever we ask, we know that we have the petitions that we have asked of Him.

And this is the confidence (the assurance, the privilege of boldness) which we have in Him: [we are sure] that if we ask anything (make any request) according to His will (in agreement with His own plan), He listens to and hears us. And if (since) we [positively] know that He listens to us in whatever we ask, we also know [with settled and absolute knowledge] that we have [granted us as our present possessions] the requests made of Him.

There are times in life when prayers go forth, but it doesn't seem like anyone is listening. We search the skies for the answer to our requests, but we come back to seek God again and wonder the reason that the time is quickly passing, but the answer has not yet arrived. Could it be that as we are waiting on God, the reality is that He is really waiting for us to believe in the One that has all that is needed and to put our confidence in Him before we receive the answer to the thing we desire? Maybe He is just wondering why we won't just simply trust Him.

Your thoughts for today:

_____
_____
_____
_____
_____
_____
_____
_____

Pastor Donell Givens

About the Author

Pastor Donell Givens received the Lord very early in his life, and even as a child, he had a burning quest to encounter God. People that spend any amount of time with him don't generally stay the same. His passion for God's presence and Word seem to infect to some degree all who regularly fellowship with him. This man has fallen deeply in love with God, and he tries intently to get others to do the same.

Pastor Givens has held almost every position in the churches he has attended over the years, from usher to choir member to deacon to associate pastor.

He is the senior pastor of *Spirit of Truth Fellowship Church* in Los Angeles, California.

He enjoys ministering one on one and to entire congregations as well.

www.ingramcontent.com/pod-product-compliance
Lightning Source LLC
Chambersburg PA
CBHW071411040426
42444CB00009B/2193